William Bradford

Discover the Life of a Colonial American

Kieran Walsh

Rourke

Publishing LLC

Vero Beach, Florida 32964

www.rourkepublishing.com

PHOTO CREDITS: All photos © North Wind Picture Archives

Title Page: *The Pilgrims land at Plymouth in 1620.*

Editor: Frank Sloan

Cover and page design by Nicola Stratford

Library of Congress Cataloging-in-Publication Data

Walsh, Kieran.
  William Bradford / Kieran Walsh.
     p. cm. -- (Discover the life of a colonial American)
  Includes bibliographical references (p.   ) and index.
  ISBN 1-59515-136-2 (hardcover)
  1. Bradford, William, 1590-1657--Juvenile literature. 2. Pilgrims (New Plymouth Colony)--Biography--Juvenile literature. 3. Governors--Massachusetts--Biography--Juvenile literature. 4. Massachusetts--History--New Plymouth, 1620-1691--Juvenile literature. 5. Plymouth (Mass.)--Biography--Juvenile literature. I. Title. II. Series: Walsh, Kieran. Discover the life of a colonial American.
  F68.B8235W55 2004
  974.4'02'092--dc22
                                                    2004009653

Printed in the USA

CG/CG

Table of Contents

Young Bradford

William Bradford was born in Yorkshire, England in 1590. Bradford's parents died when he was very young. After this, Bradford lived with relatives in different parts of England.

At the age of 12, Bradford was living in a part of England called Scrooby. It was in Scrooby that Bradford joined the **separatist** movement. The separatists wanted to separate from the Church of England because their religious beliefs were different. In 1609 the separatists left England and moved to Holland to escape religious **persecution**.

A young separatist

Life in Holland

Bradford and the separatists remained in Holland for 11 years. During this time, Bradford married a woman named Dorothy and fathered a son named John.

Life in Holland wasn't much better than in England. Work was hard to find. A war between Spain and the Netherlands was brewing. Also, King James of England encouraged the people of the Netherlands to **harass** the separatists.

King James of England sits on his throne.

Getting Ready to Leave

The leader of the separatists, John Robinson, encouraged his people to travel to America. There they could still be a part of England but worship in their own way. Their original plan was to settle in Virginia.

Along with a man named John Carver, William Bradford did a lot of work planning and preparing for this journey. It was around this time that Bradford began calling his fellow separatists **Pilgrims**.

The Pilgrims leave the Netherlands for America.

The separatists left for America on September 16, 1620. The voyage across the Atlantic was difficult. One man fell overboard. Many of the ship's crew wanted to turn back.

Storms rocked the Mayflower *on its voyage across the Atlantic.*

The Mayflower

Originally, the trip to America was going to be made on two different ships. One of the ships, though, was in poor shape. Instead, all 102 passengers traveled aboard a single vessel—the *Mayflower*.

Arriving in America

About two months later, on November 19, the Pilgrims spotted land. Two days later, they arrived at Provincetown, Massachusetts.

The Pilgrims first landed at Provincetown, Massachusetts.

Because they hadn't landed in Virginia, the Pilgrims stayed aboard the *Mayflower* for a time until they decided where they would live.

The Mayflower *anchors off the coast of Massachusetts.*

The Mayflower Compact

On November 21, 41 men—including William Bradford—signed the Mayflower Compact. This was a document that gave the Pilgrims a temporary government.

William Bradford with the Pilgrims

The Plymouth Colony

With winter approaching, William Bradford was given the task of finding a suitable area for the new colony. The site he chose was Plymouth, where the Pilgrims settled on December 26.

The first man to govern Plymouth Colony was John Carver, elected in 1620. When Carver died in 1621, William Bradford was elected governor.

It was during Bradford's first year as governor that the colony celebrated what is believed by many to be the first Thanksgiving.

Pilgrim families make their way onshore at Plymouth.

Governor of Plymouth Colony

Bradford spent most of the rest of his life as the governor of Plymouth Colony. He was reelected 30 times.

Bradford was known as a firm but fair ruler. He worked hard to create good **relations** with Native Americans and do business with other countries.

Bradford and his group finally made their home at Plymouth.

Bradford and his fellow Pilgrims made friends with Native Americans.

A Remarkable Legacy

In 1630, Bradford began writing the history of Plymouth Colony. These writings were eventually published as a book, *History of Plymouth Plantation*. It is because of Bradford's writings that we know details of the *Mayflower* voyage and the Pilgrims in early America.

William Bradford died on May 9, 1657. His death was a great loss to the people of Plymouth Colony, but he left behind a remarkable **legacy**.

A Pilgrim looks out to sea.

Important Dates to Remember

1590	Born in Yorkshire, England
1609	Moves to Holland with the separatists
1620	Sails to America on the *Mayflower*
1621	Elected governor of Plymouth Colony
1630	Begins writing *History of Plymouth Plantation*
1657	Dies in Plymouth

Glossary

harass (huh RAS) — to annoy or disturb

legacy (LEG uh see) — something handed down from a person of the past

persecution (PUR sih kyuh shun) — bothering or mistreating

Pilgrims (PIL grumz) — travelers

relations (rih LAY shunz) — the way people treat each other

separatist (SEP uh rut ust) — one who believes in separating from an established church or government

Index

Further Reading

Bjornlund, Linda D. *The Thirteen Colonies*: *Massachusetts*. Lucent, 2001

Schmidt, Gary D. *William Bradford: Plymouth's Faithful Pilgrim*.
   Eerdmans Publishing Co., 1998

Stefoff, Rebecca. *Colonial Times*: *1600-1700*. Benchmark Books, 2001

Stefoff, Rebecca. *Voices from Colonial Life*. Benchmark Books, 2003

Websites to Visit

http://www.infoplease.com/ce6/people/A0808664.html
Infoplease – William Bradford
http://pilgrims.net/plymouth/
Homepage of Plymouth, Massachusetts
http://www.plimoth.org/
Plimoth Plantation

About the Author

Kieran Walsh is a writer of children's nonfiction books, primarily on historical and social studies topics. Walsh has been involved in the children's book field as editor, proofreader, and illustrator as well as author.